DIMENSIONS OF HEALTH

COMMUNITY HEALTH

by Kurt Waldendorf

WWW.FOCUSREADERS.COM

Copyright © 2026 by Focus Readers®, Mendota Heights, MN 55120. All rights reserved. No part of this book may be reproduced or utilized in any form or by any means without written permission from the publisher.

Focus Readers is distributed by North Star Editions:
sales@northstareditions.com | 888-417-0195

Produced for Focus Readers by Red Line Editorial.

Photographs ©: Shutterstock Images, cover, 1, 4–5, 7, 8–9, 10, 15, 16–17, 20–21, 29; iStockphoto, 13, 24, 26–27; Tom Herde/The Boston Globe/Getty Images, 19; Brittany Murray/Long Beach Press-Telegram/MediaNews Group/Getty Images, 23; Red Line Editorial, 25

Library of Congress Cataloging-in-Publication Data
Library of Congress Cataloging-in-Publication Data is available on the Library of Congress website.

ISBN
979-8-88998-523-5 (hardcover)
979-8-88998-583-9 (ebook pdf)
979-8-88998-555-6 (hosted ebook)

Printed in the United States of America
Mankato, MN
082025

ABOUT THE AUTHOR
Kurt Waldendorf is the author of more than a dozen books for children. When he's not writing or editing, he enjoys indoor rock climbing and running along the shore of Lake Michigan with his dog. He lives in Chicago.

TABLE OF CONTENTS

CHAPTER 1

Fixing a Food Desert 5

CHAPTER 2

What Is Community Health? 9

CONNECTIONS

Promoting Public Health 14

CHAPTER 3

Finding Resources 17

CHAPTER 4

Making Plans 21

CHAPTER 5

Getting Involved 27

Focus Questions • 30
Glossary • 31
To Learn More • 32
Index • 32

CHAPTER 1

FIXING A FOOD DESERT

For years, a girl and her family walked to their neighborhood grocery store to buy food. But last fall, the store closed. People in the neighborhood were frustrated. It had been the area's only grocery store. Now, only fast-food restaurants and convenience stores remained. People had nowhere to

> Foods sold at convenience stores tend to be high in salt and fat.

buy fresh fruits and vegetables. The neighborhood had become a **food desert**.

In school, the girl had studied how important it was to eat fruits and vegetables. So, she took action. She talked to her parents and neighbors. Together, they made a plan. They convinced the convenience store owners to add new items. Instead of just chips, they now sold fruit, too.

A community health worker (CHW) heard about the group's efforts. He helped them. He brought flyers that people could pass out. The flyers shared facts about food deserts. They explained how a lack of nutritious food harms

Getting enough fruits and vegetables lowers people's risk for many diseases.

people's health. It raises their risks for diseases such as type 2 diabetes.

Soon other organizations got involved. A local church started a community garden. The city council met to discuss the issue. Its members talked about steps that could help. By the next year, a new grocery store had opened.

CHAPTER 2

WHAT IS COMMUNITY HEALTH?

Some types of health focus on one person's body and mind. Community health looks at people as groups. It focuses on people who live in a certain area. This area might be just one neighborhood. Or it could be a whole city. People look for ways to improve the health of everyone who lives there.

The amount of housing, transportation, and natural areas in a community shape the health of the people who live there.

Polluted water can make people sick. In some cases, it's unsafe for people to touch.

Many factors affect a community's health. Some factors are environmental. These factors have to do with people's surroundings. How much pollution an area has is one example. Other factors are social. They have to do with the groups people are part of and the **resources** they have. Race, gender, ethnicity, and wealth are social factors. People in certain groups are more likely to have health problems. For example, health care can be expensive. So, low-income people may struggle to pay for the care they need.

HEALTH DISPARITIES

A community contains different groups of people. Certain groups have higher risks for disease. These differences are called health disparities. Many health disparities are based on access to resources. Clean water and healthy food are two key resources. So is having doctors or clinics nearby. A lack of resources can cause **stress**. So can living in unsafe areas. Stress harms people's health over time.

CHWs help solve these problems. For example, they talk with community members. They learn what problems people are facing. Then they make plans to help.

Many plans have one of three goals. The first is preventing disease. Seeing a doctor regularly helps people stay healthy. But not everyone can do this. CHWs help fill the gaps. They visit people's homes. They teach people ways to stay healthy. And they help people get resources such as food and housing. Then people are less likely to get sick.

The second goal is detecting disease. Finding a disease early often helps in

Home health care is one type of social service. Workers visit people in their homes to help with treatment or daily activities.

treating it. That's why CHWs provide health screenings. They give free tests for diseases such as cancer.

The third goal is finding treatment for disease. CHWs support community members with chronic illnesses or other health problems. CHWs connect people to **social services** that can help.

CONNECTIONS

PROMOTING PUBLIC HEALTH

Community health is part of public health. Public health also focuses on groups. But it looks at larger areas. Examples include states or countries. Public health workers make plans to support the health of all people in these areas. CHWs often work to put these plans into practice.

For example, vaccines are important for public health. A vaccine helps a person's body fight a disease. This helps the person not get sick. It also protects their community. When more people are protected, it's harder for a disease to spread.

The Centers for Disease Control and Prevention (CDC) is a public health organization in the United States. It studies diseases and how they spread. The CDC creates immunization schedules. These lists show common diseases. They recommend

Measles spreads very quickly, so health experts recommend that kids get vaccinated for it before attending school.

when people should get vaccines for them. And they say how many doses people need.

CHWs tell people about these schedules. They help parents learn what vaccines their kids need. CHWs also hold immunization clinics. These events give people vaccines, sometimes for free.

CHAPTER 3

FINDING RESOURCES

Health centers are a key resource for community health. They provide care to underserved people. Underserved people have less access to resources. Examples include people without **health insurance** and people without homes. Centers give care even if people can't pay. They also help people find information.

There are more than 10,000 health centers in the United States. For some people, these clinics are the only way to get care.

Health centers are run by people from the community. So, their workers understand the issues and questions that people may have. This helps them give good advice.

Nonprofit organizations are another resource. The YMCA is one example. It

TRANSLATING

The people in a community often speak many languages. Some may struggle to talk with doctors. People may have a hard time explaining their problems. Or doctors might not understand them. This makes it hard to get the right treatment. To help, health centers provide professional translators. Translators help people and doctors communicate clearly. Then people can get the care and information they need.

A translator may go to a person's appointment and help the person speak with a doctor.

offers classes and programs that help people stay active. It provides food to kids in need. And it helps adults find jobs.

Schools play a role in community health, too. Health teachers and school nurses can answer questions. If needed, they can connect people with experts for more support.

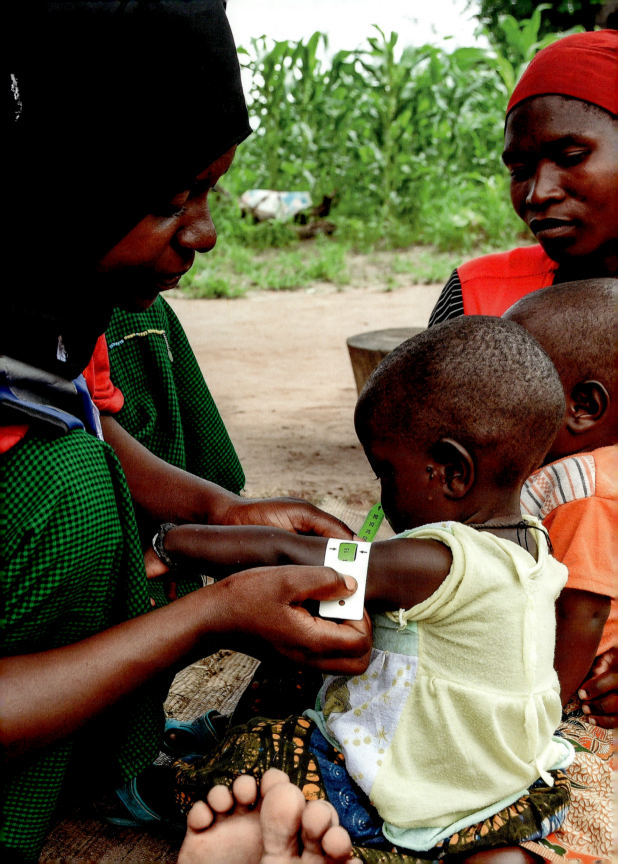

CHAPTER 4

MAKING PLANS

Improving a community's health starts with understanding its problems. To do this, CHWs often team up with local health departments. These departments are part of the government. They look out for the health of people in a city or county. Part of this work involves doing assessments. Departments gather data

▶ **A CHW in Tanzania checks children for signs of malnutrition.**

from clinics and hospitals. They also conduct **surveys**. This information helps them identify common health problems in the community. It shows which groups are most affected. It may even explain the cause.

CHWs look at the information carefully. Then they create a community health plan. This plan aims to address the biggest issues. To make plans, CHWs

HEALTH DEPARTMENTS

Health departments look out for communities in many ways. Some workers test water to make sure it is safe. Others visit restaurants, hotels, and day cares. They make sure each place follows safety rules. Workers also suggest ways to fight disease and lower pollution.

A worker presents the results of a survey done in Los Angeles County in 2024.

team up with people in the community. For example, heart disease and diabetes are top causes of death in the United States. They are also preventable in most cases. To prevent these diseases, CHWs may work with schools. They may start programs that promote healthy eating. CHWs may set up diabetes screenings at health centers. These steps lower the risk of disease.

Social workers connect people with programs that meet needs. For example, many help unhoused people find safe places to live.

CHWs also work to make communities safer. To do this, they may partner with social workers. These workers may help people find housing or treatment for **addiction**.

Every three to five years, community health plans get updated. CHWs get new data. They study this information to learn which plans worked and which didn't.

They also try to find out why. As a result, CHWs are always learning. They keep looking for ways to help everyone in the community be as healthy as possible.

THE PLANNING PROCESS

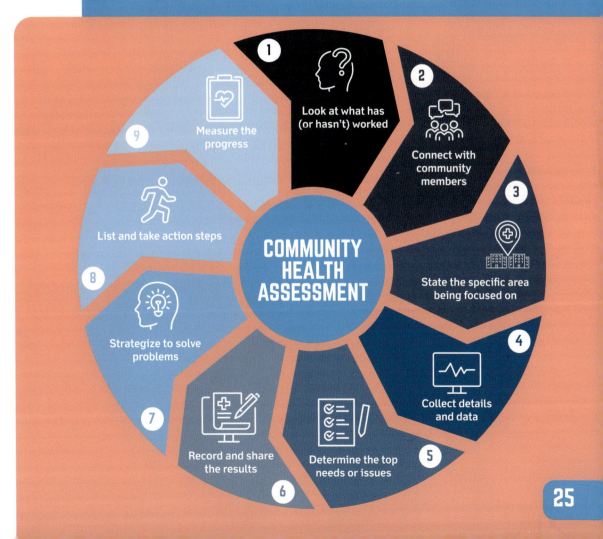

CHAPTER 5

GETTING INVOLVED

Individuals can help their communities, too. Look up the clinics and nonprofits in your area. These places often need volunteers. For example, you could pack food for people in need. Or you could visit people in hospitals or nursing homes.

Donating is another option. People can give food to a food pantry. Food pantries

Visiting people at nursing homes helps them feel less lonely. This improves their health.

help people who can't afford groceries. Shelters provide places for unhoused people to stay. People can donate money or household items.

People don't need money to make a difference. One big way to help is by encouraging others to make healthy choices. For instance, you can spend time being active outside with your friends

SPREADING SAFETY

You can model healthy choices even if you get sick. For example, you can avoid spreading germs to others. Cover your coughs and sneezes. Wash your hands often. And stay home if you throw up or have a fever. All these actions help others stay healthy.

Parks provide places for people to be active, even in cold weather.

or family. Or you can ask your school to serve healthy food at lunch.

You can also call or write local leaders. Ask them to pass laws that limit pollution. Or ask them to add more parks or green spaces. These changes can help make the community a healthier, safer place to live.

FOCUS QUESTIONS

Write your answers on a separate piece of paper.

1. Write a sentence that describes the main ideas of Chapter 4.

2. What is one thing you could do to help improve the health of your community?

3. What are environmental factors based on?

    A. the groups people are part of
    B. the resources people have
    C. people's surroundings

4. Which of these is a social factor?

    A. the number of surveys that CHWs do
    B. the amount of pollution in the air
    C. the amount of money a person has

Answer key on page 32.

GLOSSARY

addiction
A powerful need to keep doing something. An addiction may involve drugs or alcohol.

food desert
A place where people are unable to buy fresh, healthy food.

health insurance
A program that helps pay for people's health care.

nonprofit
Doing work because it is important instead of focusing on making money.

resources
Things, such as money or transportation, that help people meet needs or solve problems.

social services
Programs that help people in need by providing things such as food, housing, and medical care.

stress
A feeling of tension or pressure caused by the things going on around someone.

surveys
Lists of questions that groups send out to learn about people's thoughts and experiences.

TO LEARN MORE

BOOKS

Gaertner, Meg. *Great Careers in Health Care*. Focus Readers, 2022.

Lilley, Matt. *Inventing Vaccines*. Focus Readers, 2022.

Miller, Marie-Therese, PhD. *Jobs in Health Care*. Abdo Publishing, 2024.

NOTE TO EDUCATORS

Visit **www.focusreaders.com** to find lesson plans, activities, links, and other resources related to this title.

INDEX

Centers for Disease Control and Prevention (CDC), 14
city, 7, 9, 21
community health workers (CHWs), 6, 12–13, 14–15, 21–25

disease, 7, 11–13, 14, 22–23
donating, 27–28

environmental factors, 10

food desert, 5–6

health centers, 17–18, 23
health departments, 21–22
health insurance, 17
hospitals, 22, 27

neighborhood, 5–6, 9
nonprofit, 18, 27

resources, 11–12, 17–18

schools, 6, 19, 23, 29
shelters, 28
social factors, 10–11
social services, 13
social workers, 24
surveys, 22

translators, 18

vaccines, 14–15

Answer Key: 1. Answers will vary; 2. Answers will vary; 3. C; 4. C